EMOTIONAL SOVEREIGNTY

Master Your Emotions.
Master Your Life.

DEBORAH E. JONES

DEDICATION

This book is dedicated to every person who has ever felt overwhelmed by their emotions and wondered if peace of mind was truly possible. To those who have faced stress, conflict, loss, and uncertainty yet continued searching for clarity and strength—may these pages remind you that emotional mastery is not about suppressing what you feel but learning to guide your responses with wisdom and intention.

~Best Wishes, Deborah

I also dedicate this work to my children, who have taught me patience, resilience, and the responsibility of leading by example.

~ With all my love, Mom

And with deep gratitude, I dedicate this book to my husband, Derk, whose unwavering support, encouragement, and belief in me have been a constant source of strength throughout this journey.

~Love, Me.

ABOUT THE AUTHOR

Deborah E. Jones is a psychology student at Grand Canyon University (GCU), writer, and advocate for personal growth and emotional resilience. Through years of self-reflection, research, and study of psychology, philosophy, and self-development, she began exploring how individuals can regulate their emotions and reshape their internal narratives. Much of her own journey involved learning from books, educational resources, and self-guided study, which helped her develop the emotional awareness and discipline that inspired this work.

Deborah wrote Emotional Sovereignty with the intention of becoming the kind of guide she once wished she had during her own journey through the uncharted territory of mastering emotional regulation. Her goal is to help others recognize that the power to regulate their emotional responses already exists within them. She believes that through awareness, inner work, and intentional practice, individuals can recondition their thinking patterns and cultivate calm strength in the face of life's challenges.

"The greatest transformation begins the moment we realize the power we have been searching for outside ourselves has been within us all along."

~Deborah E. Jones

TABLE OF CONTENTS

INTRODUCTION
UNDERSTANDING EMOTIONAL SOVEREIGNTY

Most people believe that emotions simply happen to them.

A stressful conversation triggers anger. A moment of criticism produces defensiveness. An unexpected problem creates anxiety or frustration. These reactions often occur so quickly that they feel automatic, almost as if they are beyond our control.

For many people, this pattern becomes a normal part of daily life. Emotions rise, reactions follow, and only afterward do we pause to reflect on what happened. Sometimes we regret our responses. Sometimes we wonder why the situation escalated more than it should have. And sometimes we simply feel overwhelmed by the intensity of our own emotional reactions. What many people do not realize is that this pattern is not inevitable.

While emotions themselves are natural and necessary, the way we respond to them can be learned, refined, and strengthened. The ability to recognize emotional reactions and guide them with intention is a skill—one that can dramatically change the way we experience the world. This skill is what I call emotional sovereignty.

Emotional sovereignty is the ability to remain aware of your emotional experience without allowing emotions to control your behavior. It is the practice of feeling deeply while responding thoughtfully. Instead of being pulled in every direction by stress, criticism, or conflict, emotionally sovereign individuals maintain inner stability, allowing them to act with clarity and purpose. In other words, emotional sovereignty is about learning to govern your internal world rather than being governed by it.

This concept is especially important in today's world. Modern life presents a constant stream of information, expectations, and interactions that can easily overwhelm our emotional systems. Social media, professional pressure, family responsibilities, and everyday challenges often create an environment where reactions happen faster than reflection.

When emotions dominate our responses, communication becomes strained, decision-making becomes clouded, and relationships suffer. Over time, these patterns can leave people feeling exhausted, misunderstood, or disconnected from their own sense of balance. But there is another way to live.

Through awareness, reflection, and practice, individuals can develop the ability to observe emotions without becoming consumed by them. This does not mean suppressing feelings or pretending that difficult emotions do not exist. Instead, it means learning to recognize emotions as signals rather than commands.

When emotions are treated as information rather than instructions, a powerful shift occurs. Instead of reacting impulsively, we begin to respond intentionally.

Throughout this book, we will explore the principles and practices that support this transformation. You will learn how emotional reactions originate in the brain, why certain situations trigger stronger responses than others, and how our interpretations of events often intensify emotional experiences.

More importantly, you will learn practical techniques that help interrupt automatic reactions and create space for thoughtful responses. These techniques include recognizing emotional triggers, separating thoughts from feelings, reframing stressful interpretations, setting healthy boundaries, and practicing the pause principle. Each of these tools contributes to the larger goal of emotional sovereignty.

Developing emotional sovereignty does not mean becoming emotionally distant or detached from life. On the contrary, people who develop this skill often experience emotions more clearly and more authentically. The difference is that their emotions no longer dictate their actions. They are able to feel anger without becoming aggressive, to feel disappointment without losing perspective, and to face stress without becoming overwhelmed.

This capacity allows individuals to navigate relationships with greater empathy, communicate more effectively during conflict, and make decisions with clarity even in challenging situations.

Emotional sovereignty also strengthens resilience. Life inevitably includes moments of uncertainty, loss, and difficulty. When individuals possess the ability to regulate their emotional responses, they are better equipped to face these moments with steadiness and courage. Rather than feeling controlled by external circumstances, they remain anchored in their own internal balance.

The journey toward emotional sovereignty begins with awareness. Simply recognizing how emotions influence behavior is the first step toward change. From there, each skill introduced in this book builds upon the previous one, gradually strengthening the reader's ability to respond thoughtfully in situations that once triggered automatic reactions.

Like any meaningful form of growth, this process requires patience and practice. Emotional habits that developed over many years do not change overnight. However, even small shifts in awareness can produce meaningful improvements in daily life. A single moment of pause before reacting can transform a conversation. A reframed interpretation can reduce unnecessary stress. A clear boundary can protect emotional energy and preserve healthy relationships. Over time, these small changes accumulate and create lasting transformation.

This book is not about achieving perfection. Everyone experiences emotional reactions from time to time, and even the most self-aware individuals occasionally respond impulsively. Emotional sovereignty is not the absence of emotion; it is the presence of awareness and choice.

By developing this awareness, you gain the ability to guide your responses rather than be controlled by them.

In the chapters that follow, we will explore how emotional reactions occur, how they influence communication and decision-making, and how practical strategies can restore clarity and balance. Each chapter introduces tools designed to help you move from reaction to intentional response.

The goal is not to eliminate emotion from your life.

The goal is to place emotion in its proper role—as a source of information, insight, and connection rather than a force that determines your actions. When you learn to guide your emotional responses with intention, you discover a quiet but powerful truth: The greatest control we possess is not over the events that happen around us, but over how we respond to them.

That discovery is the beginning of emotional sovereignty.

"You have power over your mind—not outside events. Realize this, and you will find strength."

~ Marcus Aurelius

CHAPTER 1
THE PROBLEM: EMOTIONAL HIJACKING

Most people believe they make rational decisions throughout the day. They assume their words, reactions, and choices are guided primarily by logic and conscious thought. Yet modern psychology and neuroscience reveal something quite different: much of human behavior is driven by emotional reactions that occur before rational thinking has time to intervene.

This phenomenon explains why someone might say something in anger that they immediately regret, send an impulsive message during a heated disagreement, or decide in the middle of stress that they later recognize was not wise. In these moments, emotion has temporarily taken control of the mind.

The purpose of this chapter is to introduce the concept of emotional hijacking, explain why it happens, and begin developing awareness of the triggers that cause emotional reactions. Emotional mastery does not mean eliminating feelings. Instead, it means learning to recognize when emotions are rising and to respond with intention rather than impulse.

Understanding this process is the first step toward emotional sovereignty.

The Amygdala Hijack

In the mid-1990s, psychologist Daniel Goleman popularized the term amygdala hijack to describe what happens when emotional reactions override rational thinking. To understand this concept, it helps to briefly examine how the brain processes information. Deep within the brain sits a small almond-shaped structure called the amygdala. The amygdala plays a critical role in detecting threats and triggering emotional responses such as fear, anger, or anxiety. Its primary job is survival. When it senses danger, it activates the body's stress response almost instantly.

The amygdala operates much faster than the rational part of the brain, the prefrontal cortex, which is responsible for reasoning, planning, and decision-making. Because the amygdala evolved to help humans respond quickly to threats, it can initiate a reaction before the prefrontal cortex has time to analyze the situation.

In prehistoric times, this rapid response helped humans survive predators and other dangers. If early humans paused to logically evaluate whether a charging animal posed a threat, they might not have survived long enough to reproduce. Quick emotional responses were adaptive in dangerous environments.

However, modern life rarely involves life-or-death threats. Yet the brain's ancient survival system still reacts as if everyday stressors are emergencies. A disagreement with a coworker, criticism from a supervisor, or a rude comment online can trigger the same neurological alarm system designed for survival in the wilderness.

When the amygdala perceives a threat—whether real or perceived—it sends signals that activate the fight-or-flight response. Adrenaline and cortisol surge through the body. Heart rate increases. Muscles tense. Attention narrows.

In this state, the brain prioritizes immediate reaction rather than careful reasoning.

This is the moment when emotional hijacking occurs.

During an amygdala hijack, people may experience:

- Sudden Anger

Sudden anger during an amygdala hijack can look like someone instantly raising their voice, slamming a door, or reacting with intense frustration over something small. The emotional reaction feels immediate and overwhelming, often before the person has time to think through the situation.

- Defensiveness

Defensiveness may appear as someone quickly blaming others, interrupting, or refusing to listen to feedback. The person feels attacked, even if the conversation was meant to be constructive or calm.

- Panic

Panic can show up as rapid breathing, a racing heart, or a sense that something terrible is about to happen. The person may feel the urge to escape the situation or struggle to think clearly because their brain has shifted into survival mode.

- Impulsive Speech

Impulsive speech might look like blurting out hurtful words, speaking before thinking, or saying things that the person later regrets. In this moment, emotional reactivity overrides thoughtful communication.

- Tunnel Vision Thinking

Tunnel vision thinking occurs when someone becomes fixated on one interpretation of a situation and cannot see other perspectives. They may believe they are completely right while ignoring context, nuance, or possible solutions.

Later, when the emotional intensity fades and the rational brain regains control, many people reflect on the situation and think:

Why did I react like that?

The answer is often simple: logic was temporarily bypassed by an emotional alarm system that believed immediate action was necessary.

Recognizing this biological mechanism is important because it helps remove some of the shame people feel about their emotional reactions. Emotional responses are not signs of weakness or moral failure. They are part of the brain's natural survival system.

However, while emotional reactions are natural, they do not always lead to wise outcomes. The skill of emotional sovereignty involves learning to interrupt the hijack before it controls behavior.

Reactive Communication

One of the most common places where emotional hijacking appears is in communication. Words spoken during emotional intensity often carry more power—and more damage—than people realize. Reactive communication occurs when someone speaks from an emotional surge rather than thoughtful intention. It often happens quickly and without reflection. In these moments, people may say things they later regret.

Consider a simple example.

A colleague sends an email that seems critical of your work. Without pausing to clarify the tone or intent, you interpret the message as disrespectful. Emotion rises. Anger follows. Within minutes, you fire back a sharp reply.

Later, after the exchange escalates, you realize the colleague may not have intended criticism at all. The situation could have been clarified with a simple question. Yet the emotional reaction drove the interaction in a different direction.

Reactive communication often includes patterns such as:

- Interrupting Others

Interrupting may look like cutting someone off mid-sentence because you feel the need to defend yourself immediately. Instead of fully hearing the other person, the brain rushes to respond before the conversation is complete.

- Raising One's Voice

Raising one's voice can appear as suddenly speaking louder, sharper, or more aggressively than the situation requires. The person may not realize their tone has escalated because their emotions are driving the reaction.

- Sarcasm Or Insults

Sarcasm or insults might look like making cutting remarks such as, "Wow, thanks for the expert opinion," or belittling the other person's point. These comments are often meant to protect the speaker's pride while subtly attacking the other person.

- Defensive Language

Defensive language can sound like statements such as, "I didn't do anything wrong," or "You're always blaming me." The focus shifts from understanding the issue to protecting one's self-image.

- Impulsive Text Messages or Emails

Impulsive messages often appear as quickly typed responses sent while emotions are still high. The message may be blunt, accusatory, or poorly worded because the sender reacts before taking time to think or clarify.

These reactions are often fueled by the brain's perception of threat. When people feel criticized, rejected, or disrespected, the amygdala interprets the situation as a challenge to personal safety or status. The brain reacts quickly, preparing to defend itself.

Unfortunately, reactive communication frequently escalates conflict rather than resolving it. Words spoken in anger can damage relationships, create workplace tension, and prolong misunderstandings.

Emotionally intelligent communication, by contrast, involves a brief but powerful step: **The Pause.**

The pause creates space between emotion and response. Instead of reacting immediately, a person allows the initial emotional surge to pass before responding thoughtfully. This simple shift dramatically changes the tone of conversations and the outcomes of disagreements. The ability to pause is one of the foundational skills of emotional sovereignty.

How Stress Clouds Decision Making

Emotional hijacking is not limited to moments of anger or conflict. Chronic stress can also impair the brain's ability to think clearly and make sound decisions. When stress levels remain elevated for extended periods, the body stays in a constant state of physiological alertness. Cortisol, the primary stress hormone, remains elevated in the bloodstream. Over time, this affects cognitive functioning.

Research shows that high stress can reduce activity in the prefrontal cortex, the part of the brain responsible for:

- **Reasoning**

When stress is high, the brain's ability to logically analyze situations becomes weaker. People may jump to conclusions, misinterpret events, or struggle to think through problems clearly.

- **Impulse Control**

Stress reduces the brain's ability to pause before reacting. As a result, individuals may act quickly on emotions such as anger, frustration, or fear without thinking about the consequences.

- **Long-term Planning**

Under high stress, the brain shifts its focus to immediate survival or short-term relief rather than to future outcomes. This can lead to decisions that feel good in the moment but may not support long-term goals.

- **Ethical Decision Making**

Stress can narrow a person's perspective, making it harder to consider fairness, values, and the impact of choices on others. When emotional pressure is high, decisions may be driven more by urgency or self-protection than thoughtful moral judgment.

At the same time, stress increases activity in the amygdala, which heightens emotional sensitivity. The result is a brain that becomes more reactive and less reflective.

In practical terms, stress can lead to:

- **Impulsive Decisions**

When stress activates the amygdala, the brain prioritizes immediate emotional responses rather than thoughtful reflection. This can cause people to make quick decisions driven by frustration, fear, or anger rather than carefully considering their options.

- **Difficulty Concentrating**

Heightened emotional stress can make it harder for the brain to focus on tasks or process information clearly. As a result, individuals may feel distracted, mentally scattered, or unable to complete tasks that normally require attention.

- ## **Overreaction to Minor Problems**

When the amygdala becomes more active, small challenges can feel larger and more threatening than they actually are. This can lead to emotional responses that are stronger than the situation truly requires.

- ## **Difficulty Seeing Long-term Consequences**

Stress shifts the brain's focus toward immediate emotional relief rather than future outcomes. Because of this, individuals may overlook how their reactions or decisions could affect them later.

For example, someone experiencing financial stress may make rushed spending decisions or risky investments out of fear. A person overwhelmed at work might respond harshly to colleagues even when no harm was intended.

Stress narrows attention. Instead of considering multiple perspectives or possible solutions, the mind becomes focused on immediate relief from discomfort.

This is why emotional mastery requires more than simply controlling anger in isolated moments. It also involves managing overall stress levels and maintaining mental clarity under pressure. Practices such as mindfulness, reflective journaling, and structured pauses during emotional intensity help restore balance between the emotional brain and the rational brain.

When the mind is calm, the prefrontal cortex can engage fully, allowing people to evaluate situations with greater clarity.

Why Emotional Mastery Matters

Emotional mastery is not about suppressing feelings or becoming detached from human experience. Emotions carry valuable information. They signal when something matters, when boundaries are crossed, or when a situation requires attention. However, when emotions dictate behavior without reflection, they can lead to consequences that undermine personal goals and relationships. Learning emotional mastery provides several powerful benefits.

First, it improves decision-making. When people can observe emotions without immediately reacting, they gain access to the rational thinking needed to carefully evaluate choices.

Second, emotional mastery strengthens relationships. Calm communication reduces unnecessary conflict and helps people express their needs clearly without escalating tension.

Third, emotional mastery enhances resilience. Life inevitably presents challenges, disappointments, and unexpected changes. Individuals who can regulate emotional reactions are better equipped to adapt to difficult circumstances without becoming overwhelmed.

Finally, emotional mastery supports personal leadership. Whether in professional settings, family life, or community roles, individuals who remain calm under pressure inspire confidence and stability in others.

Emotional sovereignty does not eliminate emotion; it places emotion in its proper role. Feelings become signals to observe rather than forces that dictate behavior.

Exercise: Trigger Awareness Journal

The first step toward emotional sovereignty is awareness. Before you can manage emotional reactions, you must understand what triggers them.

Over the next week, begin keeping a Trigger Awareness Journal.

Each time you notice a strong emotional reaction, write down the following:

What happened?

Describe the situation briefly.

What emotion did you feel?

Examples might include anger, frustration, embarrassment, anxiety, or sadness.

What thoughts occurred in that moment?

Write the automatic thoughts that arose.

How did you react?

Did you speak immediately? Withdraw? Raise your voice?

How might you respond differently next time?

The goal of this exercise is not self-criticism. Instead, it is about identifying patterns. Most people discover that their emotional reactions follow predictable themes. Certain situations consistently trigger strong responses, often tied to past experiences or deeply held beliefs. By identifying these patterns, you gain the first layer of control over them. Awareness turns unconscious reactions into conscious choices.

Emotional hijacking is a universal human experience. Everyone, regardless of intelligence or maturity, occasionally reacts before thinking. The difference between reactive living and emotional sovereignty lies in the ability to recognize these moments and gradually shift from impulse to awareness.

In the next chapter, we will explore the emotional body itself, how emotions arise, what they communicate, and how you can observe them without becoming overwhelmed by them.

Emotional mastery begins not with control, but with understanding.

"It's not what happens to you, but how you react to it that matters." ~Epictetus

CHAPTER 2
UNDERSTANDING THE EMOTIONAL BODY

In the previous chapter, we explored how emotional hijacking occurs—how the brain's threat detection system can override logic and push us into reactive behavior before we have time to think. That understanding is an important first step, but it raises an equally important question:

What exactly are emotions, and why do they arise so quickly?

To develop emotional sovereignty, we must first understand the nature of the emotional body. Emotions are not enemies to be suppressed, nor are they forces that must be obeyed without question. They are signals—complex biological and psychological messages that convey information about our environment, beliefs, and internal needs.

Many people struggle with emotions, not because they feel too much, but because they have never been taught how to observe emotions without becoming overwhelmed by them. When emotions arise, the natural tendency is to either react immediately or attempt to suppress the feeling entirely. Neither approach leads to emotional clarity. Emotional sovereignty lies in a third path: awareness without immediate reaction.

In this chapter, we will explore how emotions form, what they communicate, and how you can begin to observe them with curiosity rather than being controlled by them.

What Is the Emotional Body?

The term emotional body refers to the system through which humans experience and process emotions. While emotions are felt psychologically, they are also deeply connected to physical processes in the brain and body.

Every emotion involves three interconnected components:

- A physiological response in the body

Every emotion begins with a physical response in the body, such as changes in heart rate, breathing, muscle tension, or the release of stress hormones like adrenaline and cortisol. These bodily reactions prepare the nervous system to respond quickly to perceived danger, excitement, or emotional stimulation.

- A cognitive interpretation in the mind

After the body reacts, the brain interprets what the emotion means by evaluating the situation and attaching meaning to it. This mental interpretation helps determine whether the feeling is understood as anger, fear, sadness, or joy based on past experiences and beliefs.

- A behavioral impulse to act

Emotions naturally create an urge to take action, such as defending oneself, withdrawing, expressing feelings, or seeking support. This behavioral impulse is the outward expression of the emotional experience and often drives how a person responds to others in the moment.

When these three elements combine, the experience of emotion emerges.

For example, imagine receiving unexpected criticism during a meeting. Within seconds, your heart rate may increase, your muscles may tense, and your breathing may become shallow. This is the physiological response.

At the same time, your mind interprets the event. You might think, "They are disrespecting me," or "Everyone thinks I am incompetent." These thoughts intensify emotional reactions.

Finally, the emotion produces an impulse to act. You might feel the urge to defend yourself, argue, withdraw, or shut down entirely.

This entire process often unfolds within seconds.

Understanding this sequence is important because it reveals that emotions are not random events. They are structured experiences that follow identifiable patterns. When we learn to recognize those patterns, we gain the ability to influence how we respond.

Emotions as Information

One of the most important shifts in emotional mastery is learning to view emotions as information rather than commands. Every emotion carries a message.

Anger often signals that a boundary feels violated. Fear alerts us to potential danger. Sadness may indicate loss or unmet expectations. Anxiety can signal uncertainty about the future. These signals are valuable. Without them, humans would struggle to navigate social relationships, avoid threats, or recognize meaningful opportunities.

However, problems arise when people treat emotions as instructions that must be acted upon immediately.

For instance, feeling angry does not necessarily mean you must confront someone. Feeling anxious does not always mean a situation is truly dangerous. Feeling rejected does not always mean someone intended harm. Emotions provide data, but they do not always provide accurate conclusions.

Consider the difference between emotion and interpretation.

You might feel a surge of anxiety before giving a presentation. The emotion signals that the situation feels important and uncertain. However, the interpretation of that anxiety might vary. One person might interpret it as excitement or motivation, while another might interpret it as evidence that failure is inevitable.

The emotional signal is the same, but the interpretation determines the outcome. Learning to separate the emotional signal from the interpretation is a key step toward emotional sovereignty.

Why Emotions Feel So Overwhelming

Many people struggle with emotions because they believe emotions must either be fully expressed or completely suppressed. This false choice creates a cycle of reactivity and avoidance. Part of the reason emotions feel overwhelming is that they are felt in the body before they are processed in the mind. When an emotional trigger occurs, physical sensations often appear first. You may notice a tightening in the chest, warmth in the face, or a heaviness in the stomach.

These sensations are the body's early warning signals. If we immediately attach stories to these sensations—This is terrible, this person is attacking me, I cannot handle this—the emotional intensity increases rapidly.

But if we learn to observe the sensations without attaching immediate judgment, something remarkable happens: the emotion begins to lose its overwhelming power. This does not mean the emotion disappears. Instead, it becomes an experience to be observed rather than an event to be acted upon. Mindfulness practitioners sometimes describe this as "surfing the wave of emotion." Like a wave in the ocean, emotions rise, peak, and eventually fall if we allow them to move naturally.

When we resist emotions or amplify them through interpretation, the wave becomes larger and more difficult to navigate.

The Observer Mind

A central skill in emotional mastery is developing what psychologists sometimes call the observer mind. The observer mind is the ability to step back internally and notice thoughts and emotions as experiences rather than identities.

Instead of saying, I am angry, the observer mind might say, I notice anger arising.

This subtle shift creates psychological distance. When you identify completely with an emotion, it feels as though the emotion defines you in that moment. Anger becomes your entire reality. Fear becomes your entire focus. But when you observe the emotion, you remember that the emotion is simply one experience within a larger awareness.

Think of it like watching clouds pass through the sky. The clouds may be dark or light, fast-moving or slow. But the sky itself remains stable. Your awareness functions in a similar way. Emotions move through the mind like weather patterns, but awareness remains the stable background in which those emotions occur.

Practicing the observer's mind does not eliminate emotions. Instead, it allows you to experience them without losing perspective.

Emotional Waves and Time

Another important insight into emotions is that they are temporary. Research on emotional processing suggests that the physiological component of an emotion typically lasts about ninety seconds if it is not reinforced by continued thoughts or rumination. What extends emotional reactions beyond that initial surge is often the mental narrative that follows.

For example, if someone insults you, the initial emotional reaction may last only a short time. However, if you replay the event repeatedly—thinking about what was said, imagining what others might think, and anticipating future confrontations—the emotional reaction can continue for hours or even days. The mind feeds the emotion through continued interpretation. Learning to recognize this pattern allows you to interrupt it. When you notice yourself repeatedly replying to a triggering event, you can ask a simple question:

Is this thought helping me understand the situation, or am I simply reliving the emotion?

This question often creates the pause necessary to disengage from unproductive mental loops.

The Difference Between Suppression and Observation

A common misconception about emotional regulation is that it requires suppressing emotions. Suppression means pushing feelings out of awareness and pretending they do not exist. While suppression may appear effective in the short term, it often leads to greater emotional intensity later. Suppressed emotions tend to resurface in unexpected ways—through irritability, stress, or physical tension.

Observation is different.

Observation means acknowledging the presence of an emotion without immediately acting on it or attempting to eliminate it.

For example, if you feel frustrated during a conversation, you might silently note the feeling while continuing to listen. You do not deny the frustration, but you also do not allow it to dictate your response.

This approach respects the emotional signal while preserving rational control.

Emotional Curiosity

One of the most powerful tools for observing emotions is curiosity. Instead of judging an emotion as good or bad, you can approach it with interest.

Ask questions such as:

What triggered this emotion?

What belief might be connected to it?

What need might it be signaling?

Curiosity transforms emotional experiences into opportunities for insight.

For example, if you notice repeated frustration in certain interactions, curiosity might reveal that the frustration stems from an unspoken expectation or boundary. Recognizing that pattern allows you to address the underlying issue rather than reacting to each individual event.

Curiosity replaces judgment with understanding.

Practicing Emotional Observation

Developing the observer mind requires practice. Like any skill, emotional awareness becomes stronger with repetition. A simple exercise to begin strengthening this skill involves pausing briefly whenever a noticeable emotion arises.

During the pause, ask yourself three questions:

What emotion am I experiencing right now?

Where do I feel this emotion in my body?

What thought is connected to this emotion?

By answering these questions, you create a moment of awareness between the emotional signal and your response.

This small space is where emotional sovereignty begins.

The Beginning of Emotional Sovereignty

Understanding the emotional body changes how we relate to our internal experiences. Instead of feeling controlled by emotions, we begin to see them as signals that can be observed, interpreted, and responded to with intention.

Emotions will always be part of human life. They add richness to relationships, motivate action, and help us navigate complex social environments. But when emotions become the sole driver of behavior, they can lead us away from our goals and values.

Emotional sovereignty does not mean eliminating emotions. It means placing awareness between emotion and action. That space allows you to respond with clarity rather than impulse.

In the next chapter, we will explore one of the most practical steps in emotional mastery: identifying the specific triggers that activate emotional reactions and learning how to anticipate them before they take control.

"The happiness of your life depends upon the quality of your thoughts." ~Marcus Aurelius

CHAPTER 3
IDENTIFYING EMOTIONAL TRIGGERS

In the previous chapter, we explored the emotional body—how emotions arise, how they move through the body and mind, and how awareness allows us to observe them without becoming overwhelmed. Understanding the emotional system is an important foundation, but emotional sovereignty requires a more practical skill: identifying the specific events, words, or situations that activate strong emotional responses.

These activators are known as emotional triggers.

Triggers are not inherently negative. They simply represent the moments when the emotional brain reacts quickly and intensely. Some triggers are obvious, such as direct criticism or confrontation. Others are subtle and may only become clear through reflection. A tone of voice, a certain type of question, or even a familiar situation can activate an emotional response before we realize what is happening.

Many people assume that emotions appear randomly, but emotional reactions usually follow recognizable patterns. Once those patterns are identified, individuals gain the ability to anticipate emotional reactions and respond with greater awareness. Recognizing triggers does not eliminate emotional responses, but it dramatically increases the ability to manage them.

This chapter focuses on identifying those patterns so that emotional reactions no longer occur without warning.

What Is an Emotional Trigger?

An emotional trigger is any stimulus that activates a strong emotional response. Triggers can be external events, such as a comment from another person, or internal experiences, such as a memory or thought.

Triggers often involve situations that the brain interprets as threatening to important aspects of self: personal identity, safety, belonging, or self-worth. Because the emotional brain evolved to detect threats quickly, it reacts rapidly whenever it perceives something that resembles past danger or discomfort.

For example, someone who has experienced repeated criticism may develop a heightened sensitivity to feedback. Even neutral suggestions may feel like personal attacks. Another person who values independence may feel strong frustration when they perceive others attempting to control their decisions.

In these situations, the emotional response may feel automatic. The person might react defensively before they have time to evaluate whether the situation truly requires that level of reaction.

Triggers operate much like shortcuts in the brain. Instead of evaluating each situation carefully, the brain compares the current event to previous experiences. If it finds similarities, it activates the emotional response associated with those earlier events. While this process can sometimes protect us, it can also lead to reactions that are stronger than the present situation requires.

Recognizing triggers helps us slow down this automatic pattern.

Common Categories of Emotional Triggers

Although each person's emotional triggers are unique, many triggers fall into several common categories. Recognizing these categories can help individuals begin identifying their own patterns.

- Criticism and Judgment

People who are sensitive to criticism and judgment may notice that they react strongly when receiving feedback, corrections, or differing opinions, even when the intention is helpful. Recognizing this pattern often begins by observing moments when feelings of defensiveness, embarrassment, or anger arise quickly, signaling that the brain may be interpreting the situation as a personal attack rather than neutral feedback.

One of the most powerful emotional triggers involves perceived criticism. Humans are highly sensitive to evaluation because social acceptance has historically been important for survival. When someone feels judged or criticized, the brain may interpret the situation as a threat to belonging or status.

This can lead to reactions such as defensiveness, anger, or withdrawal. Even constructive feedback may trigger these responses if a person associates criticism with past negative experiences.

- Rejection and Exclusion

Rejection and exclusion may show up as feelings of hurt, sadness, or insecurity when someone perceives they are being left out, ignored, or not valued. A person might withdraw from the situation, overanalyze social interactions, or assume others do not want them around, even when the exclusion may not have been intentional.

Humans are social beings, and feelings of rejection can activate strong emotional reactions. Being ignored, excluded from a group, or experiencing perceived rejection can trigger sadness, anxiety, or anger.

Interestingly, research shows that social rejection activates similar brain regions as physical pain. This may explain why emotional reactions to rejection can feel intense and immediate.

* Loss of Control

Loss of control may appear as frustration, irritability, or anxiety when situations do not go as planned or when someone feels powerless over an outcome. A person might try to regain control by becoming overly rigid, argumentative, or attempting to micromanage the situation or others around them.

Many people experience strong emotional responses when they feel that their autonomy is threatened. Situations that involve unexpected changes, imposed rules, or perceived manipulation may trigger frustration or resistance.

For individuals who value independence, loss of control can be one of the most significant emotional triggers.

* Uncertainty and Ambiguity

Uncertainty and ambiguity can appear as anxiety, restlessness, or mental overthinking when someone does not have clear information about what will happen next. A person may repeatedly seek reassurance, imagine worst-case scenarios, or feel uncomfortable making decisions without clear direction.

Not all triggers involve direct confrontation. Situations involving uncertainty—such as waiting for important news, navigating unclear expectations, or facing unpredictable outcomes—can trigger anxiety.

The human brain often prefers clear information, even when that information is negative. Uncertainty can prompt the mind to imagine worst-case scenarios, intensifying emotional reactions.

- Disrespect or Injustice

Disrespect or injustice may show up as intense frustration, anger, or a strong urge to defend oneself when a person feels they have been treated unfairly or dismissed. Someone might respond by confronting the situation directly, raising their voice, or becoming highly focused on correcting what they perceive as wrong.

Many individuals have strong emotional responses when they perceive unfairness or disrespect. Feeling undervalued, ignored, or treated unjustly can activate anger or indignation. This trigger is especially common among people who hold strong values around fairness, integrity, and personal dignity.

Recognizing which of these categories resonates most strongly can provide valuable insight into personal emotional patterns.

The Role of Past Experiences

Emotional triggers rarely develop in isolation. They are often shaped by previous experiences that left a lasting emotional imprint. For example, someone who grew up in an environment where mistakes were harshly criticized may develop a strong reaction to any form of evaluation later in life. Another person who experienced betrayal may become highly sensitive to signs of dishonesty.

These patterns do not mean that individuals are weak or overly sensitive. They simply reflect the brain's attempt to protect itself from repeating painful experiences. However, when past experiences influence present reactions too strongly, the emotional brain may respond to situations that no longer require protection.

Understanding the connection between past experiences and present triggers allows individuals to respond with greater compassion toward themselves. Instead of judging emotional reactions, they can begin to explore the underlying patterns that produced them.

This exploration is a key step toward emotional sovereignty.

The Moment Before Reaction

One of the most valuable insights about emotional triggers is that there is usually a small window of time between the trigger and the reaction. This window may only last a few seconds, but it provides an opportunity for awareness.

During this moment, the emotional brain has detected a potential threat, but the rational brain has not yet fully processed the situation. If individuals can learn to recognize the early signs of emotional activation—such as increased heart rate, muscle tension, or rapid thoughts—they can pause before reacting.

This pause allows the rational brain to engage and evaluate the situation more accurately. For example, imagine someone receiving a message that initially feels insulting. The emotional reaction begins immediately. However, if the person notices their emotional response and pauses before replying, they may realize that the message could be interpreted in multiple ways.

Instead of reacting defensively, they might ask for clarification. That small pause can transform the entire interaction.

Mapping Your Personal Triggers

Because emotional triggers are deeply personal, identifying them requires honest reflection. One of the most effective ways to identify triggers is to examine patterns in past reactions.

Consider moments when you've experienced strong emotional responses. Ask yourself the following questions:

1.   What was happening just before the emotion appeared?

2.   What words, actions, or situations were involved?

3.   What did the emotion seem to be protecting or defending?

Over time, these reflections often reveal consistent patterns. You may notice that certain types of interactions consistently produce frustration, while others evoke anxiety or defensiveness. Once these patterns become clear, they lose some of their power. The next time a similar situation occurs, you may recognize the trigger before the emotional reaction fully develops.

This recognition provides an opportunity to choose a more intentional response.

Anticipating Triggers

Emotional mastery does not require eliminating triggers entirely. Instead, it involves anticipating them and preparing thoughtful responses.

For example, if you know that criticism tends to trigger defensiveness, you can prepare strategies for receiving feedback more calmly. This might include asking clarifying questions, taking a moment to breathe before responding, or reminding yourself that feedback is often intended to improve outcomes rather than attack personal character. If uncertainty triggers anxiety, you might practice focusing on what you can control rather than attempting to predict every possible outcome.

Anticipation allows you to approach challenging situations with awareness rather than surprise.

Trigger Awareness Exercise

To strengthen your ability to recognize emotional triggers, begin practicing the following exercise over the next week.

Each time you notice a strong emotional reaction, write down:

1.   The situation that occurred

2.   The emotion you experienced

3.   The thought that appeared immediately after the trigger

4.   The action you took in response

5.   A possible alternative response

After several days of recording these experiences, review your notes and look for patterns.

You may discover that certain themes appear repeatedly. These themes represent the emotional triggers that most strongly influence your reactions.

Recognizing these patterns is one of the most empowering steps in emotional mastery.

Awareness as the First Layer of Control

Emotional triggers do not disappear overnight. However, awareness changes how we relate to them. When triggers operate unconsciously, they control behavior without warning. But when triggers become visible, they lose some of their automatic power. You begin to recognize the early signals of emotional activation. Instead of being surprised by your reactions, you become curious about them.

This curiosity creates space for choice. Emotional sovereignty does not mean that triggers will never arise again. It means that when they do, you are no longer powerless in their presence.

In the next chapter, we will explore one of the most powerful skills in emotional mastery: learning to separate thoughts from emotions so that feelings no longer dictate the stories we tell ourselves about a situation.

“We suffer more often in imagination than in reality.”

~ Seneca

35

CHAPTER 4
SEPARATING THOUGHTS FROM EMOTIONS

In the previous chapter, we explored emotional triggers—those moments when certain situations, words, or memories activate strong emotional responses. Recognizing triggers is an important step toward emotional mastery, but awareness alone is not always enough to prevent emotional reactions from influencing behavior. The next skill in developing emotional sovereignty is learning to separate thoughts from feelings.

For many people, emotions and thoughts appear to be the same thing. When an emotion arises, the mind automatically creates a story about why that emotion exists. The story feels convincing because it arrives quickly and seems to explain the feeling. However, the story is not always accurate.

Learning to separate thoughts from feelings allows individuals to observe emotional experiences without automatically accepting the conclusions that accompany them. This distinction is one of the most powerful tools in cognitive psychology and emotional regulation.

When you understand the difference between a feeling and the thoughts that interpret it, you gain the ability to question the story your mind is telling you. This ability creates space between emotional reaction and rational evaluation.

That space is where emotional sovereignty begins.

The Difference Between Feelings and Thoughts

At first glance, feelings and thoughts may appear inseparable. But they are actually two distinct mental processes. Feelings are emotional experiences that arise in response to events or perceptions. They are typically felt in the body and often emerge quickly. Examples of feelings include anger, sadness, fear, excitement, embarrassment, or frustration.

Thoughts, by contrast, are mental interpretations or judgments about what is happening. Thoughts attempt to explain the emotional experience. For example, imagine someone receives a brief message from a colleague that reads, "We need to talk."

The emotional reaction might be anxiety or concern. That feeling arises quickly, perhaps accompanied by a tightening in the chest or an increase in heart rate. Almost immediately, the mind begins generating thoughts to explain the feeling. The person might think, "I must have done something wrong," or "They are going to criticize my work." Notice that the emotion—anxiety—appears first. The thoughts that follow attempt to interpret the situation. However, the interpretation is not necessarily correct. The colleague might simply want to discuss a project update or share new information.

This example illustrates how easily thoughts can amplify emotional reactions. When we assume our thoughts are factual rather than interpretive, emotions gain additional intensity. Recognizing the difference between feelings and thoughts allows us to question those interpretations.

Why the Mind Creates Emotional Narratives

The human brain is designed to search for meaning. When emotions arise, the brain instinctively attempts to identify the cause. This process happens quickly because understanding the source of emotional signals historically helped humans respond effectively to threats or opportunities.

If early humans felt fear in the presence of a predator, identifying the cause quickly allowed them to take protective action. Over time, the brain evolved to generate explanations for emotional signals almost instantly.

However, modern environments are far more complex than the survival situations that shaped this system. Many emotional reactions now occur in social or psychological contexts rather than physical threats.

As a result, the mind sometimes produces explanations that are incomplete or inaccurate.

For instance, if someone appears distant during a conversation, the mind might interpret the situation as rejection or disapproval. But the person may simply be distracted or preoccupied with unrelated concerns. The emotional narrative fills in missing information, often based on past experiences rather than present evidence. This tendency does not mean the brain is malfunctioning. It simply reflects the mind's attempt to make sense of emotional signals as quickly as possible. The challenge arises when we accept these interpretations without questioning them.

Emotional Reasoning

One of the most common thinking patterns that blurs the line between thoughts and feelings is known as emotional reasoning. Emotional reasoning occurs when individuals assume that because they feel something strongly, the feeling must reflect objective reality.

For example:

- I feel anxious, so something bad must be about to happen.

- I feel offended, so that person must have meant to disrespect me.

- I feel rejected, so I must not be valued.

In each of these examples, the emotion becomes the evidence for the conclusion.

However, emotions do not always provide accurate information about the external world. They reflect internal perceptions, which may be influenced by stress, past experiences, or incomplete information.

Recognizing emotional reasoning allows individuals to pause and ask an important question:

•	Is this emotion providing useful information, or is it leading me toward an assumption?

•	This question creates an opportunity to separate the emotional experience from the interpretation that follows.

The Power of Cognitive Distance

Separating thoughts from feelings creates what psychologists sometimes call cognitive distance. Cognitive distance is the ability to step back from immediate interpretations and observe them as mental events rather than unquestionable truths.

For example, instead of thinking:

They ignored me because they must dislike me.

You might say:

I noticed that they might dislike me.

This subtle shift may seem small, but it changes the relationship between you and the thought. Instead of accepting the interpretation automatically, you recognize it as a possibility rather than a fact. This distance allows the rational brain to evaluate the situation more carefully. Cognitive distance also reduces emotional intensity. When thoughts are treated as observations rather than certainties, the emotional reaction often becomes less overwhelming.

The Thought–Emotion Cycle

Thoughts and emotions influence each other continuously. This interaction is often described as a thought–emotion cycle. An event occurs. An emotional reaction arises. The mind generates thoughts that interpret the event. Those thoughts then reinforce or amplify the emotion.

For example:

1. A coworker fails to greet you in the morning.

2. You feel slight discomfort or uncertainty.

3. The mind thinks, they must be upset with me.

4. The emotion intensifies into anxiety or frustration.

The cycle can continue as the mind generates additional interpretations:

Maybe I said something wrong yesterday.

These thoughts reinforce emotional reaction even though they may not reflect the actual situation. Breaking this cycle requires recognizing when interpretations are occurring and questioning their accuracy.

Practicing Thought Awareness

One of the most effective ways to separate thoughts from feelings is to practice identifying thoughts as they occur. Whenever you experience a strong emotion, ask yourself the following questions:

1. What emotion am I feeling right now?

2. What thought is accompanying this emotion?

3. Is this thought a fact or an interpretation?

For example, if you feel angry after receiving criticism, the thought might be, "They are trying to humiliate me." By labeling this statement as an interpretation rather than a fact, you create room to consider alternative explanations.

Perhaps the criticism was intended to improve the project. Perhaps the other person communicated poorly but did not intend harm. The goal is not to deny emotional reactions but to prevent interpretations from escalating them unnecessarily.

Reframing the Narrative

Once thoughts and feelings are separated, the next step is learning how to reframe interpretations. Reframing involves examining whether there are alternative explanations for a situation. Often, multiple interpretations are possible, and the first one the mind generates is not always the most accurate. For example, imagine someone cancels plans at the last minute. The initial thought might be, they do not respect my time.

However, alternative explanations might include unexpected obligations, personal stress, or simple forgetfulness. Reframing does not require assuming positive intentions in every situation. Instead, it encourages balanced thinking that considers multiple possibilities. This balanced approach reduces emotional escalation and supports more thoughtful responses.

The Practice of Naming Emotions

Another powerful technique for separating thoughts from feelings involves simply naming the emotion that arises.

Instead of immediately analyzing the situation, pause and say to yourself:

1. I notice frustration.

2. I notice disappointment.

3. I notice anxiety.

Research suggests that labeling emotions can reduce their intensity. When the brain identifies and names an emotional experience, the rational regions of the brain become more active, helping regulate the emotional response.

This process allows you to acknowledge the emotion without being consumed by it.

Exercise: The Thought and Feeling Log

To strengthen the ability to separate thoughts from feelings, begin practicing the following exercise. Whenever a strong emotional reaction occurs, record the experience using three simple columns:

Emotion

Identify the emotion you felt.

Thought

Write the thought that appeared alongside the emotion.

Alternative Interpretation

Consider at least one other possible explanation for the situation.

For example:

Emotion: Anxiety

Thought: My supervisor is disappointed in me.

Alternative interpretation: My supervisor may simply want to discuss the project.

This exercise trains the mind to recognize interpretations as flexible rather than fixed. Over time, the ability to evaluate thoughts becomes more natural.

Emotional Sovereignty and Clear Thinking

Separating thoughts from feelings is one of the most transformative skills in emotional mastery. When individuals learn to distinguish between emotional signals and the stories attached to them, they gain greater clarity in decision-making. Instead of reacting to interpretations that may not reflect reality, they respond to situations with greater awareness and balance. Emotions remain present, but they no longer dictate the narrative.

This shift creates a more stable inner environment where thoughts can be examined, emotions can be acknowledged, and responses can be chosen intentionally.

In the next chapter, we will explore how to reshape interpretations more effectively through a process known as cognitive reframing, a technique that allows individuals to transform stressful situations into opportunities for clarity and growth.

"People are disturbed not by things, but by the view they take of them." ~ Epictetus

CHAPTER 5
COGNITIVE REFRAMING

In the previous chapter, we explored the difference between thoughts and feelings and how the mind often creates narratives to explain emotional experiences. We learned that emotions arise quickly, and the brain generates interpretations that attempt to make sense of those emotions. These interpretations can feel convincing because they appear automatically, but they are not always accurate reflections of reality.

Once individuals begin separating thoughts from feelings, the next step is to learn how to intentionally reshape those interpretations. This skill is known as cognitive reframing.

Cognitive reframing is the process of examining the way we interpret a situation and consciously choosing a more balanced or constructive perspective. It does not involve denying reality or pretending that difficult experiences are pleasant. Instead, it involves recognizing that multiple interpretations of a situation may exist and selecting the interpretation that promotes clarity, resilience, and thoughtful action.

In many ways, cognitive reframing is the bridge between emotional awareness and emotional sovereignty. When individuals learn to reframe their interpretations, they gain the ability to transform stressful experiences into opportunities for insight and growth.

How Interpretations Shape Emotional Experience

Every experience we have passes through a filter of interpretation. When an event occurs, the brain quickly assigns meaning to that event. The meaning we assign determines the emotional response that follows. Consider a simple scenario: you send a message to a friend and do not receive a response for several hours.

The event itself is neutral: a message has not yet been answered. However, the interpretation may vary widely depending on the thoughts that arise.

One person might think they must be busy.

Another might think they are ignoring me.

A third might think, perhaps they are upset with me.

Each interpretation produces a different emotional response. The first may produce patience or neutrality. The second may produce frustration or anger. The third may produce anxiety or self-doubt. The external event remains the same, but the emotional experience changes depending on the interpretation.

This pattern occurs constantly in daily life.

Many emotional reactions are not caused solely by events themselves but by the meaning we assign to those events. Cognitive reframing allows individuals to step back and examine whether their interpretation is the most accurate or helpful one available.

The Influence of Cognitive Bias

Our interpretations are often influenced by cognitive biases—mental shortcuts the brain uses to process information quickly. These shortcuts can be useful, but they sometimes distort how we interpret situations. One common bias is confirmation bias, the tendency to search for evidence that supports existing beliefs.

For example, if someone believes they are often judged by others, they may interpret neutral comments as criticism because those interpretations confirm their expectations.

Another bias is catastrophic thinking, where the mind automatically imagines the worst possible outcome. When faced with uncertainty, the brain may jump to conclusions that exaggerate potential threats.

For instance, receiving constructive feedback at work might lead someone to think, "My supervisor must be unhappy with my performance," which then escalates to "I might lose my job." In reality, the feedback may simply reflect a normal process of improving work quality.

Cognitive reframing helps individuals recognize when biases are influencing their interpretations and replace those distortions with more balanced thinking.

Recognizing Automatic Thoughts

The first step in cognitive reframing is identifying automatic thoughts. Automatic thoughts are the immediate interpretations that appear in response to an event. They often arise so quickly that individuals may not realize they are interpreting a situation rather than observing it objectively.

For example, if a colleague speaks abruptly during a meeting, the automatic thought might be that they are disrespecting me. The emotional response might be irritation or anger. However, the colleague's behavior could have multiple explanations.

They might be under stress, distracted, or simply speaking quickly without intending disrespect. Recognizing automatic thoughts allows individuals to pause and evaluate whether their initial interpretation is accurate.

One helpful question to ask during this pause is:

What evidence supports this interpretation, and what evidence might suggest another explanation?

This question shifts attention from assumption to analysis.

Challenging the First Interpretation

Many people assume their first interpretation of an event must be correct because it feels convincing. However, the first interpretation is often shaped by emotional reactions rather than objective evaluation.

Cognitive reframing encourages individuals to challenge their initial interpretation by considering alternative possibilities. For instance, imagine receiving a short response to an email that simply says, "Noted."

The automatic thought might be:

Are they annoyed with me?

However, alternative interpretations might include:

- They are responding quickly between tasks.
- They intended to acknowledge the message briefly.
- They are currently focused on another priority.

Each interpretation leads to a different emotional response. By exploring alternative explanations, individuals reduce the likelihood of escalating emotional reactions based on assumptions. This process does not require assuming positive intentions in every situation. Instead, it promotes balanced thinking that recognizes multiple possibilities.

Reframing Stressful Situations

Cognitive reframing can be particularly powerful when applied to stressful or challenging experiences. When difficulties arise, the mind often focuses on the negative aspects of the situation.

While acknowledging challenges is important, focusing exclusively on negative interpretations can amplify emotional distress. Reframing involves identifying potential lessons, opportunities, or alternative perspectives within difficult experiences.

For example, losing an opportunity—such as a job or a project—may initially lead to disappointment or frustration. These emotions are natural. However, reframing the situation might involve recognizing that the experience provides valuable information about future goals or priorities.

Similarly, receiving criticism may feel uncomfortable, but reframing can transform that feedback into an opportunity for growth and improvement.

Reframing does not eliminate discomfort, but it changes the role discomfort plays in the experience. Instead of being purely negative, challenges become part of the process of learning and development.

The Role of Language in Reframing

The language we use when describing experiences plays a significant role in shaping interpretation.

Certain phrases reinforce negative interpretations, such as:

"This always happens to me."

"Nothing ever works out."

"They are trying to make me look bad."

These statements often involve generalizations or assumptions about others' intentions. Reframing language involves replacing these statements with more precise and balanced descriptions.

For example:

Instead of "This always happens to me," consider "This situation did not work out the way I hoped."

Instead of "They are trying to make me look bad," consider "Their comment felt critical, but I need more information before drawing conclusions."

This shift in language helps prevent interpretations from escalating emotional reactions.

Reframing and Personal Responsibility

An important aspect of cognitive reframing involves recognizing where personal responsibility lies within a situation. When individuals feel powerless, they often interpret events as entirely outside their control. This perspective can lead to frustration or helplessness. Reframing encourages individuals to identify the aspects of a situation they can influence.

For example, if a conversation becomes tense, one person cannot control the other person's behavior. However, they can control their own tone, responses, and boundaries. By focusing on what can be influenced rather than what cannot, individuals regain a sense of agency. This shift supports emotional sovereignty because it emphasizes intentional action rather than reactive behavior.

Cognitive reframing also encourages individuals to pause and examine the story they are telling themselves about a situation. Often, emotional reactions are intensified not only by the event itself but by the meaning we attach to it. For example, a delayed response from someone may be interpreted as disrespect or rejection when it could simply be a matter of timing or misunderstanding.

Reframing invites a person to ask questions such as, "What else could this mean?" or "Is there another perspective I have not considered?" This process does not dismiss real emotions; rather, it helps separate facts from assumptions.

Personal responsibility becomes clearer when individuals recognize that while they cannot control others' thoughts, reactions, or intentions, they can choose how they interpret events and how they respond. Over time, practicing reframing strengthens emotional regulation, allowing individuals to respond with greater clarity, patience, and self-control instead of reacting impulsively in emotionally charged moments.

Practicing Cognitive Reframing

Developing the skill of cognitive reframing requires consistent practice. Like any mental habit, it becomes easier with repetition.

When a stressful situation occurs, consider the following steps:

1. *Identify the emotion you are experiencing.*

2. *Notice the automatic thought that accompanies the emotion.*

3. *Ask whether the thought represents a fact or an interpretation.*

4. *Generate at least one alternative interpretation.*

5. *Choose the interpretation that allows you to respond with clarity and purpose.*

6. *Pause before responding.*

7. *Decide on a response that aligns with your values.*

8. *Reflect on the outcome afterward.*

This process does not require forcing yourself to believe an interpretation that feels unrealistic. Instead, it involves recognizing that multiple perspectives may exist and selecting the one that supports constructive action.

This approach encourages mental flexibility rather than rigid thinking about a situation. Over time, practicing this skill helps individuals respond more thoughtfully, reducing emotional reactivity and strengthening their ability to navigate challenging interactions with greater balance and self-awareness.

Exercise: The Reframing Practice

Over the next week, practice cognitive reframing by recording situations that produce strong emotional reactions.

For each situation, write down:

- **Event**

What happened?

- **Automatic Thought**

What interpretation appeared immediately?

- **Emotion**

What feeling accompanied that thought?

- **Alternative Interpretation**

What other explanation might exist?

- **Response**

How could you respond from a more balanced perspective?

Reviewing these reflections over time often reveals patterns in how the mind interprets events. The more frequently individuals practice reframing, the more naturally the mind begins to question automatic interpretations.

Clarity Through Perspective

Cognitive reframing does not eliminate difficult emotions or guarantee that every situation will be positive. Instead, it equips individuals with the ability to examine interpretations before allowing them to shape emotional reactions. By recognizing that thoughts are interpretations rather than absolute truths, individuals gain the freedom to choose perspectives that support resilience, understanding, and thoughtful action. This freedom represents an important step toward emotional sovereignty.

Clarity through perspective helps individuals slow the automatic cycle between thoughts, emotions, and reactions. By pausing to examine their interpretations, people begin to recognize how quickly the mind can draw conclusions from limited information. This awareness creates space for more balanced thinking and emotional regulation. Instead of reacting defensively, individuals can approach situations with curiosity and reflection. Over time, this strengthens emotional intelligence and improves communication with others.

People become less likely to misinterpret intentions and more likely to ask questions or seek understanding. As a result, situations that could escalate into conflict can instead become opportunities for growth, clarity, and more thoughtful responses.

In the next chapter, we will explore another essential component of emotional mastery: establishing healthy boundaries and protecting emotional energy, which allows individuals to maintain balance in relationships and environments that might otherwise drain their emotional resources.

"You have power over your mind — not outside events. Realize this, and you will find strength." ~Marcus Aurelius

CHAPTER 6
BOUNDARIES AND EMOTIONAL ENERGY

In the previous chapter, we explored cognitive reframing and how the interpretations we assign to situations influence our emotional responses. By learning to examine and reshape those interpretations, individuals gain greater clarity and emotional balance.

However, emotional sovereignty involves more than managing internal thought patterns. It also requires learning how to interact with the external world in ways that protect emotional well-being. One of the most important skills in this process is establishing healthy boundaries.

Boundaries are the guidelines we create to define what behaviors we will accept, how we expect to be treated, and how we choose to invest our time and emotional energy. They help us maintain balance in relationships and environments that might otherwise overwhelm us.

Many people struggle with boundaries because they associate them with conflict or rejection. In reality, healthy boundaries do not isolate us from others. Instead, they allow relationships to function with greater respect, clarity, and mutual understanding.

In this chapter, we will explore how boundaries work, why they are essential for emotional mastery, and how to establish them in ways that protect emotional energy while maintaining healthy connections with others.

Understanding Emotional Energy

Before discussing boundaries, it is helpful to understand the concept of emotional energy. Emotional energy refers to the mental and emotional resources we use to process experiences, respond to challenges, and engage with others. Just as physical energy can be depleted through exertion, emotional energy can be drained through prolonged stress, conflict, or overwhelming responsibilities.

When emotional energy becomes depleted, individuals may experience:

- Irritability

Irritability may look like it is becoming easily frustrated over small inconveniences or reacting more sharply than usual in conversations. A person might feel constantly on edge, snapping at others, or feeling annoyed by situations that normally would not bother them.

- Mental Fatigue

Mental fatigue often manifests as a sense of mental heaviness or feeling emotionally and cognitively drained. Tasks that usually feel manageable may suddenly require more effort, and the person may struggle to stay mentally engaged.

- Difficulty Concentrating

Difficulty concentrating can show up as trouble focusing on conversations, tasks, or reading material. The mind may wander frequently, making it hard to complete work or remember important details.

- Reduced Patience

Reduced patience may look like feeling easily overwhelmed by delays, questions, or interruptions. A person might feel rushed or irritated when things take longer than expected.

- Emotional Overwhelm

Emotional overwhelm occurs when feelings become so intense that it is difficult to process or respond calmly. A person may feel like everything is "too much," leading to withdrawal, shutting down, or emotional outbursts.

These experiences often signal that the emotional system has been overextended.

Many people attempt to manage emotional exhaustion by pushing through it. They continue responding to every demand placed upon them, often ignoring the signs that their internal resources are becoming depleted.

Without boundaries, emotional energy becomes vulnerable to constant external demands. Boundaries help regulate how emotional energy is distributed.

What Boundaries Are—and What They Are Not

A boundary is a clear statement of what you are willing to accept and what you are not willing to accept in a particular situation. It communicates your limits in a way that protects your time, energy, and emotional well-being.

Healthy boundaries help others understand how to interact with you respectfully while also allowing you to maintain a sense of balance and self-respect. When expressed clearly and consistently, boundaries create healthier relationships by reducing confusion, resentment, and emotional exhaustion.

Boundaries can involve:

Time

Communication

Responsibilities

Emotional Availability

Physical Space

For example, a boundary might involve declining additional commitments when your schedule is already full or expressing that certain types of communication are not acceptable. It is important to recognize what boundaries are not.

Boundaries are not attempts to control other people's behavior. You cannot force others to change how they act. Instead, boundaries define how you will respond if certain behaviors occur. For instance, you cannot require someone to always agree with you, but you can establish a boundary that conversations must remain respectful.

Healthy boundaries focus on personal responsibility rather than controlling others.

Why Boundaries Feel Difficult

Many individuals struggle to establish boundaries because they fear disappointing others or creating tension in relationships. Social conditioning often teaches people to prioritize harmony and approval, sometimes at the expense of personal well-being.

People who have difficulty setting boundaries may experience patterns such as:

- Agreeing to commitments they do not have time for

- Tolerating disrespectful behavior to avoid confrontation

- Feeling responsible for other people's emotions

- Suppressing personal needs to maintain relationships

These patterns may provide short-term comfort by avoiding conflict, but they often lead to long-term emotional exhaustion. When boundaries are absent, emotional energy becomes vulnerable to constant demands and expectations.

Learning to establish boundaries requires recognizing that personal well-being is not selfish. Protecting emotional energy allows individuals to show up in relationships with greater patience, clarity, and authenticity.

Emotional Boundaries in Relationships

Relationships often provide the greatest opportunities for connection and support, but they can also become sources of emotional strain when boundaries are unclear. Emotional boundaries help individuals maintain a sense of identity within relationships. They allow people to care about others without absorbing their emotions or becoming responsible for solving every problem.

For example, a friend may share a difficult experience and seek support. Offering empathy and listening attentively can strengthen the relationship. However, emotional boundaries prevent the listener from becoming overwhelmed by the situation or feeling responsible for fixing it. Healthy emotional support involves compassion without over-identification.

Similarly, emotional boundaries help individuals recognize when conversations or interactions become harmful. If someone repeatedly uses criticism, manipulation, or disrespectful language, boundaries allow individuals to express that such behavior is unacceptable. This does not necessarily end the relationship. Instead, it creates an opportunity for healthier interaction.

Protecting Time and Attention

One of the most practical forms of boundaries involves protecting time and attention. Modern environments are filled with constant demand messages, notifications, requests, and obligations. Without boundaries, these demands can consume significant emotional energy.

Protecting time may involve practices such as:

- Scheduling uninterrupted periods for focused work or reflection

- Limiting exposure to environments that create unnecessary stress

- Declining commitments that do not align with personal priorities

Many people feel uncomfortable declining requests, particularly when they want to be helpful. However, agreeing to every request often leads to resentment or burnout.

When individuals learn to evaluate whether a commitment aligns with their values and capacity, they become more intentional about how they invest their time. Boundaries help ensure that time and attention are directed toward what matters most.

Recognizing Energy-Draining Patterns

Certain patterns in relationships and environments consistently drain emotional energy. Recognizing these patterns allows individuals to respond more intentionally.

Examples of energy-draining patterns include:

- Repeated criticism without constructive purpose

- Conversations that revolve around negativity or conflict

- Expectations that one person must always accommodate others

- Environments where boundaries are consistently ignored

Not every challenging interaction requires withdrawal, but awareness of these patterns allows individuals to evaluate whether certain dynamics need adjustment.

In some cases, boundaries may involve limiting the frequency or duration of interactions that consistently drain emotional energy.

In other cases, boundaries may involve communicating expectations clearly so that interactions become more balanced.

Communicating Boundaries Clearly

Establishing boundaries requires clear communication. When expectations remain unspoken, others may not realize that certain behaviors are problematic.

Effective boundary communication is typically:

- Calm

Communicating boundaries calmly means expressing your limits without yelling, blaming, or becoming emotionally reactive. Staying calm helps the other person focus on the message rather than reacting defensively to your tone.

- Direct

Being direct means clearly stating what you need or what behavior you will or will not accept. Direct communication avoids hints, passive comments, or expecting others to guess your boundaries.

- Respectful

Respectful boundary communication means speaking to others with dignity while also valuing your own needs. It focuses on the behavior or situation rather than attacking the person.

- Specific

Being specific means clearly describing the exact behavior that is acceptable or unacceptable. Specific boundaries reduce confusion and make it easier for others to understand and respect your expectations.

For example, instead of saying, "You are always interrupting me," a clearer statement might be:

This approach focuses on the desired behavior rather than attacking the other person's character. Similarly, if someone repeatedly requests additional commitments when your schedule is full, a boundary might be expressed as:

"I appreciate the opportunity, but I cannot take on additional responsibilities right now."

Communicating boundaries calmly reinforces emotional sovereignty by demonstrating that personal needs can be expressed without hostility.

The Emotional Impact of Boundaries

When individuals begin establishing boundaries, they may initially experience discomfort. This discomfort often arises because the behavior represents a shift from previous patterns. Others may respond with surprise if they are accustomed to a different dynamic. However, healthy boundaries often lead to more balanced relationships over time.

In many cases, people respect boundaries once they are communicated clearly and consistently. Boundaries also reduce resentment by preventing situations in which individuals agree to commitments they do not truly want to accept.

By protecting emotional energy, boundaries allow individuals to engage with others more authentically.

Boundaries and Self-Respect

At a deeper level, boundaries reflect self-respect. When individuals recognize that their time, attention, and emotional well-being have value, they become more intentional about how they share those resources. Self-respect does not require perfection or constant control over emotions. Instead, it involves acknowledging personal limits and honoring them.

Boundaries are a practical expression of that respect.

Practicing Boundary Awareness

Developing healthy boundaries begins with self-awareness.

Consider reflecting on the following questions:

1.   In which situations do I feel emotionally drained?

2.   Are there commitments I regularly accept even though they create stress?

3.   Are there interactions where I feel my needs are not being respected?

4.   What boundaries might help create a healthier balance?

These reflections can reveal areas where emotional energy is being depleted unnecessarily. Once these patterns become visible, individuals can begin experimenting with small adjustments. Even minor changes in communication or scheduling can significantly improve emotional balance.

Exercise: Boundary Reflection

To strengthen awareness of emotional boundaries, try the following exercise.

Over the next week, notice situations where you feel emotionally drained or overwhelmed. When these situations occur, write down:

- The interaction or environment involved

- The emotion you experienced

- The behavior or expectation that contributed to the feeling

- A boundary that might improve the situation

For example, if a conversation repeatedly becomes critical or stressful, a possible boundary might involve limiting the duration of the conversation or redirecting the topic. This exercise helps transform vague discomfort into specific insights about how emotional energy can be protected.

The Balance Between Connection and Protection

Healthy boundaries do not isolate individuals from relationships or responsibilities. Instead, they create a balance between connection and protection. Without boundaries, emotional energy becomes vulnerable to constant external demands. With overly rigid boundaries, individuals may withdraw from meaningful relationships.

Emotional sovereignty involves finding a balance where connection remains possible while emotional well-being is preserved. This balance allows individuals to engage with others from a place of stability rather than exhaustion.

Moving Toward Emotional Sovereignty

Boundaries represent a crucial step in emotional mastery because they extend emotional awareness into real-world interactions. By defining which behaviors are acceptable and how they will invest emotional energy, individuals take responsibility for maintaining their internal balance.

Over time, practicing boundaries becomes less uncomfortable and more natural. Individuals begin to recognize that protecting emotional energy allows them to contribute more effectively to both personal and professional environments.

In the next chapter, we will explore another powerful tool for emotional mastery: the pause principle, a simple yet transformative practice that creates space between emotional triggers and responses, allowing individuals to respond thoughtfully rather than react impulsively.

"He who is brave is free." ~Seneca

CHAPTER 7
THE PAUSE PRINCIPLE

Throughout this book we have explored the mechanisms behind emotional reactions. We examined how the brain's threat-detection system can hijack our thinking, how emotions arise in the body, how triggers activate automatic responses, and how our thoughts shape the stories we tell ourselves about events.

Now we arrive at one of the most powerful tools in emotional mastery:

The pause principle.

The pause principle is deceptively simple. It is the practice of creating a brief moment of awareness between an emotional trigger and your response. Yet within that small moment lies the difference between reacting impulsively and responding with clarity.

Most emotional conflicts occur not because people intend harm, but because reactions happen too quickly. Words are spoken before the mind has time to evaluate them. Messages are sent before emotions settle. Decisions are made under the influence of stress rather than thoughtful reflection.

The pause principle interrupts this pattern.

By learning to pause before responding, you allow the rational brain to re-engage and evaluate the situation. This shift may last only a few seconds, but those seconds can transform the outcome of a conversation, a decision, or even an entire relationship.

Emotional sovereignty begins with this simple but profound skill.

Why We React So Quickly

To understand the power of the pause, we must first revisit why emotional reactions occur so rapidly.

The human brain evolved to detect threats quickly and respond immediately. The amygdala—part of the brain responsible for processing emotional signals—acts as an early warning system. When it perceives potential danger, it activates the body's fight-or-flight response.

This response prepares the body to act. Heart rate increases, muscles tense, and attention narrows toward the perceived threat.

While this system was crucial for survival in early human environments, it can create challenges in modern life. Today, most emotional triggers involve social interactions rather than physical threats. Yet the brain reacts with the same urgency.

A critical email, an argument, or a moment of embarrassment may trigger the same physiological reaction that once helped humans escape predators.

The emotional system moves quickly. The rational brain, the prefrontal cortex—requires a little more time.

The pause principle simply gives the rational brain the time it needs.

The Small Window of Choice

Between every stimulus and response exists a small window of choice.

This window is often so brief that people do not notice it. Emotional reactions appear instantaneous because the brain processes triggers quickly.

However, with practice, this window becomes easier to recognize.

Imagine someone criticizing your work during a meeting. The emotional reaction might include irritation or defensiveness. The automatic impulse may be to interrupt, argue, or defend your position immediately.

If you pause—even for a moment—you create an opportunity to evaluate the situation.

You may realize that the criticism contains useful information. You may decide to ask clarifying questions rather than respond defensively. Or you may choose to address the issue calmly after the meeting.

Without the pause, reaction controls the outcome. With the pause, choice becomes possible.

Emotional Momentum

Emotions behave much like momentum. When they begin moving quickly, they tend to accelerate unless something interrupts them.

A single critical comment can quickly escalate into an argument if both individuals react immediately. Each reaction fuels the next emotional surge. The pause principle interrupts this momentum.

When one person pauses rather than reacting, the emotional escalation often slows. The conversation shifts from confrontation to reflection. The pause does not eliminate emotion, but it prevents emotion from controlling the direction of the interaction.

The Neuroscience of the Pause

The effectiveness of the pause principle is supported by neuroscience.

When emotional triggers activate the amygdala, the brain enters a heightened state of alert. During this state, the rational brain temporarily loses influence. However, even a brief pause—combined with slow breathing—can begin restoring balance.

Slow breathing activates the parasympathetic nervous system, which signals the body to relax. As the physiological stress response decreases, activity in the prefrontal cortex increases.

This shift allows the brain to move from reaction toward reasoning.

In other words, pausing gives the brain time to transition from emotional alarm to thoughtful evaluation.

The Three Stages of the Pause

The pause principle involves three simple stages:

Notice

Breathe

Respond

Each stage strengthens emotional awareness and prevents automatic reactions from taking control.

Notice

The first stage involves recognizing the emotional signal. This may appear as a physical sensation such as tension in the chest, a rapid heartbeat, or a sudden surge of frustration.

Learning to notice these signals is essential. They serve as early indicators that an emotional trigger has occurred.

When you recognize these signals, you know it is time to pause.

Breathe

The second stage involves slowing your breathing.

Taking a slow breath interrupts the body's stress response. It sends a signal to the nervous system that the situation does not require immediate action.

This brief physiological shift gives the rational brain time to engage.

Respond

The final stage involves choosing a response intentionally.

Instead of reacting automatically, you evaluate the situation and decide how to proceed. This might involve asking a question, expressing your thoughts calmly, or choosing to revisit the conversation later.

The key difference is that the response is deliberate rather than impulsive.

The Pause in Communication

Communication provides one of the most powerful opportunities to apply the pause principle. Many conflicts escalate because people respond immediately when emotions are high. Words spoken during these moments often carry more intensity than intended.

The pause creates an opportunity to consider how your response will affect the conversation.

Before speaking, ask yourself:

- What outcome do I want from this conversation?

- Will my response move the conversation closer to that outcome?

This reflection often leads to calmer and more constructive communication.

The Pause in Decision Making

The pause principle also improves decision-making.

Stress often pressures individuals to make quick decisions. While some situations require rapid action, many decisions benefit from reflection.

Pausing allows individuals to evaluate options more carefully and consider long-term consequences.

This practice is particularly useful when facing decisions involving:

- Financial Choices

Pausing before making a financial decision allows you to consider whether the purchase or investment aligns with your long-term goals. Instead of acting on impulse, you give yourself time to evaluate risks, benefits, and potential consequences.

- Professional Opportunities

Taking a moment to pause when presented with a new opportunity allows you to reflect on whether the decision supports your career path and personal values. This pause helps ensure that choices are based on thoughtful evaluation rather than pressure or excitement in the moment.

- Relationship Conflicts

Pausing during a disagreement allows emotions to settle before responding. This brief moment can prevent reactive words and create space for a calmer, more constructive conversation.

- Major Life Transitions

When facing significant life changes, pausing allows you to consider how the decision will affect your future and overall well-being. Taking time to reflect helps you move forward with clarity rather than reacting to uncertainty or external pressure.

A brief pause can prevent decisions driven purely by emotional urgency.

Practicing the Pause

Like any skill, the pause principle becomes stronger with practice.

Begin by applying it in small, everyday situations. When someone interrupts you, when traffic becomes frustrating, or when a message triggers irritation, practice pausing before reacting.

Over time, the pause becomes more natural.

The goal is not to eliminate emotional reactions entirely. Instead, the goal is to become aware of those reactions early enough to prevent them from controlling behavior.

Exercise: The Ten-Second Pause

For the next week, practice the following exercise whenever you notice an emotional reaction beginning to rise.

1.   Notice the emotion.

2.   Take a slow breath.

3.   Count slowly to ten before responding.

During those ten seconds, observe the emotion without acting on it. Often, the emotional intensity will decrease enough to allow a more thoughtful response.

The Pause as a Habit

With consistent practice, the pause principle becomes a habit rather than a deliberate effort.

Instead of reacting automatically, the mind learns to slow down when emotional triggers occur. Conversations become calmer. Decisions become clearer. Conflicts become easier to navigate.

This shift does not require perfection. Everyone occasionally reacts impulsively.

However, each time you practice the pause, you strengthen your ability to respond with clarity rather than impulse.

Emotional Sovereignty in Action

Emotional sovereignty does not mean living without emotion. Emotions are part of human experience and provide valuable information about what matters to us.

However, emotional sovereignty ensures that emotions inform behavior rather than control it. The pause principle provides the practical mechanism for achieving this balance.

Within the brief space between trigger and response lies the ability to choose how you engage with the world.

In the next chapter, we will explore how emotional sovereignty becomes a daily practice—one that integrates awareness, boundaries, reframing, and the pause principle into a consistent way of living with clarity and calm strength.

"You always own the option of having no opinion."

~ Marcus Aurelius

CHAPTER 8

EMOTIONAL SOVEREIGNTY

Living With Calm Authority in a Reactive World

Throughout this book, we have explored the inner mechanics of emotional life. We examined how emotional hijacking occurs, how the emotional body functions, how triggers activate automatic responses, and how the mind constructs interpretations that shape our reactions. We learned how cognitive reframing changes perspective, how healthy boundaries protect emotional energy, and how the pause principle creates space between stimulus and response.

Each of these practices represents an essential component of emotional mastery.

But emotional mastery is not the final destination.

The deeper goal is something far more powerful: emotional sovereignty.

Emotional sovereignty is the state in which a person remains aware of their emotional experiences without being controlled by them. It is the ability to feel deeply while responding intentionally. It allows individuals to engage with the world calmly, even when circumstances are chaotic or unpredictable.

In a society where reactions often dominate conversations and conflicts escalate quickly; emotional sovereignty becomes a form of quiet leadership. Those who develop this skill bring stability to environments that might otherwise become overwhelmed by emotion.

What Emotional Sovereignty Means

The word sovereignty traditionally refers to independence or self-governance. When applied to emotional life, it describes the ability to guide one's own internal state rather than being governed by external events.

Emotional sovereignty does not mean that a person becomes indifferent or detached from the world. On the contrary, emotionally sovereign individuals often experience emotions deeply. What distinguishes them is their ability to observe those emotions without losing control of their actions.

Instead of reacting impulsively, they respond deliberately.

Instead of becoming overwhelmed by stress or criticism, they evaluate situations with clarity.

Instead of allowing other people's behavior to dictate their emotional state, they maintain internal balance.

Emotional sovereignty is not a trait that some people are born with and others lack. It is a skill that develops through awareness and practice. The techniques explored in previous chapters—recognizing triggers, reframing interpretations, setting boundaries, and practicing the pause—are all components of this larger capacity.

Together, they create a framework for living with emotional independence.

The Reactive World We Live In

To understand the importance of emotional sovereignty, consider the environment in which modern individuals operate.

Information moves rapidly. Communication occurs instantly through digital platforms. Opinions are expressed publicly and often impulsively. In many spaces, emotional reactions spread quickly and intensify collective tension.

In such an environment, reacting emotionally has become almost automatic. People often respond to situations immediately rather than pausing to reflect.

The result is a culture where:

- **Conversations Escalate Quickly**

Without pausing to reflect, people often respond immediately to emotional triggers during discussions. This can cause disagreements to intensify rapidly, turning simple conversations into heated conflicts.

- **Misunderstandings Multiply**

When individuals react quickly instead of listening carefully, they may misinterpret what others are saying. These misunderstandings can grow over time, creating unnecessary tension and confusion in relationships.

- **Stress Spreads Easily Through Social Interaction**

Emotional reactions can influence the tone and mood of an entire interaction. When one person responds with frustration or anxiety, those emotions can quickly spread to others involved in the conversation.

Within this environment, emotional sovereignty becomes increasingly valuable.

When one person remains calm while others react impulsively, that calmness often shifts the tone of the entire interaction. Emotional stability can interrupt cycles of escalation and create space for thoughtful dialogue.

In this way, emotional sovereignty becomes not only a personal skill but also a social contribution.

This final chapter brings together the principles of this book into a unified philosophical, practical approach to living with clarity, composure, and emotional authority.

The Inner Architecture of Emotional Sovereignty

Emotional sovereignty rests on several foundational principles. These principles guide how individuals relate to their emotions, thoughts, and interactions with others.

- **Awareness**

The first pillar of emotional sovereignty is awareness.

Without awareness, emotional reactions occur automatically. Individuals may not recognize triggers or thought patterns until after they have already reacted.

Awareness allows individuals to notice emotional signals as they arise. By observing physical sensations, emotional shifts, and automatic thoughts, people become conscious participants in their emotional experience.

Awareness is the gateway to choice.

- **Interpretation**

The second pillar involves interpretation.

Events themselves do not determine emotional responses; interpretations do. By examining the stories, the mind creates about events, individuals gain the ability to reshape those narratives.

Cognitive reframing transforms interpretations that intensify emotional distress into perspectives that promote clarity and resilience.

- **Boundaries**

The third pillar involves boundaries.

Emotional sovereignty requires protecting the internal environment. Boundaries define how emotional energy is invested and prevent external demands from overwhelming personal well-being.

Healthy boundaries allow individuals to remain compassionate without sacrificing their own stability.

- **Pause**

The fourth pillar is the pause principle.

The pause is the moment when emotional sovereignty becomes possible. It interrupts automatic reactions and allows the rational mind to engage before action occurs. This brief space between trigger and response is where intentional choice emerges.

Emotional Authority

Emotional sovereignty ultimately leads to emotional authority, the ability to remain composed even when external circumstances become difficult.

Emotionally sovereign individuals often display certain qualities:

They listen carefully before responding.

They remain calm during disagreement.

They acknowledge emotions without becoming overwhelmed by them.

They communicate boundaries respectfully and clearly.

These qualities often inspire trust in both personal and professional relationships. When individuals demonstrate emotional authority, others feel safer expressing their perspectives because conversations remain grounded rather than reactive.

Emotional authority does not require dominating discussions or controlling others. It emerges naturally from internal stability.

Compassion Without Absorption

One common misunderstanding about emotional regulation is that maintaining composure requires emotional detachment from others. However, emotional sovereignty does not eliminate empathy or compassion.

In fact, emotional sovereignty strengthens compassionate engagement because it prevents individuals from becoming overwhelmed by others' emotions.

When emotional boundaries are clear, people can support others without absorbing their distress.

For example, a friend experiencing a difficult situation may share their concerns. An emotionally sovereign listener can offer empathy, encouragement, and thoughtful advice without becoming consumed by the situation themselves.

This balance allows individuals to remain present and supportive while preserving their emotional stability.

Responding Rather Than Reacting

At the heart of emotional sovereignty lies a fundamental shift: moving from reaction to response.

Reactions are immediate and often driven by emotional momentum. Responses, by contrast, are intentional and guided by reflection.

Consider two individuals receiving the same criticism.

The first reacts defensively, raising their voice and arguing immediately.

The second pauses, considers the feedback, and asks clarifying questions.

Both individuals experienced the same emotional trigger. The difference lies in how they responded.

The pause created space for the second individual to choose a response aligned with their goals rather than reacting impulsively.

This distinction illustrates the essence of emotional sovereignty.

Emotional Sovereignty and Personal Leadership

Emotional sovereignty also contributes to personal leadership.

Leadership is not limited to formal positions of authority. It appears that whenever individuals influence the tone and direction of interactions.

Emotionally sovereign individuals often serve as stabilizing forces in groups because they remain composed during challenging situations.

Their presence can reduce tension, encourage thoughtful discussion, and prevent conflicts from escalating unnecessarily.

By regulating their own emotional responses, they help create environments where others feel comfortable expressing ideas and perspectives.

This form of leadership emerges naturally from emotional stability.

Integrating the Practices

The practices explored throughout this book function together as a system.

Awareness reveals emotional signals.

Trigger recognition anticipates reactions.

Thought separation distinguishes feelings from interpretations.

Cognitive reframing reshapes perspectives.

Boundaries protect emotional energy.

The pause interrupts impulsive reactions.

Together, these skills cultivate emotional sovereignty.

Like any form of mastery, emotional sovereignty develops gradually through consistent practice. Each moment of awareness strengthens the capacity for thoughtful response.

Over time, the internal landscape becomes calmer and more stable.

A Daily Practice

Emotional sovereignty is not a destination reached once and maintained effortlessly. It is an ongoing practice that evolves throughout life.

Each day provides opportunities to practice awareness, reframing, and intentional response. Some days will feel easier than others. Emotional challenges will still arise.

However, the difference lies in how those challenges are approached.

Instead of feeling controlled by emotional reactions, individuals begin to recognize that they possess the capacity to guide their responses.

This realization transforms emotional experiences from obstacles into opportunities for growth.

The Quiet Strength of Emotional Sovereignty

In a world where many interactions occur at high emotional intensity, calm presence becomes a powerful form of strength.

Emotionally sovereign individuals do not need to dominate conversations or react to every challenge. Their stability speaks for itself.

They understand that emotions are signals, not commands. They allow feelings to inform their understanding without allowing those feelings to dictate behavior.

This balance creates clarity in moments where others might feel overwhelmed.

A Final Reflection

At the beginning of this journey, we examined how easily emotions can hijack the mind. We explored how automatic reactions emerge and how interpretations shape emotional experiences.

Through awareness, reflection, and practice, those reactions can be transformed.

Emotional sovereignty does not eliminate emotion, it elevates it. Emotions become guides rather than drivers.

When individuals cultivate this ability, they discover a quiet but powerful truth:

The greatest control we possess is not over the world around us, but over how we respond to it.

This realization marks the beginning of a life guided by clarity, resilience, and calm authority.

And that is the essence of emotional sovereignty.

"No man is free who is not master of himself." ~ Epictetus

Living With Emotional Sovereignty

Emotions are a natural part of the human experience, yet many people spend their lives feeling as though their emotions control them. Stressful situations arise, reactions happen quickly, and only afterward do we reflect on what we might have said or done differently. This cycle of reaction often becomes a habit that shapes communication, decisions, and relationships. The purpose of this book has been to show that emotional reactions do not have to dictate the course of our lives. With awareness and practice, individuals can learn to guide their responses with greater clarity and intention.

Throughout this book, we explored how emotional hijacking occurs and why the brain sometimes reacts before logic has time to engage. Understanding this process helps us approach emotional reactions with curiosity instead of frustration. We also examined how emotions arise in the body and why they serve as signals rather than problems to be eliminated. When emotions are understood as information rather than commands, they become easier to navigate. This shift in perspective is the first step toward emotional sovereignty.

Recognizing emotional triggers is another important step in developing emotional awareness. Many of our reactions are influenced by patterns formed through past experiences and repeated behaviors. When similar situations occur, those patterns activate automatically and shape how we respond. By identifying these triggers, we gain the ability to anticipate emotional responses rather than be surprised by them. Awareness creates the opportunity to respond with intention instead of reacting automatically.

We also explored how thoughts and emotions work together to influence our experiences. The interpretations we create about situations often intensify emotional responses, especially when those interpretations are negative or incomplete. Learning to separate thoughts from feelings allows us to examine the stories we tell ourselves more carefully. Through cognitive reframing, stressful situations can be viewed with greater perspective and clarity. This ability to reshape interpretation is a powerful tool for emotional balance.

Healthy boundaries play an essential role in maintaining emotional stability. Without boundaries, emotional energy can become drained by constant demands, conflict, or environments that create unnecessary stress. Boundaries help individuals protect their time, attention, and emotional well-being. They allow us to remain compassionate and supportive without absorbing every emotional current around us. Establishing boundaries creates the space necessary for emotional clarity and balance.

The pause principle is perhaps the simplest and most transformative skill discussed in this book. By creating even, a brief moment between an emotional trigger and a response, we allow the rational mind to engage before action occurs. That small pause interrupts automatic reactions and opens the door for thoughtful decision-making. Over time, practicing the pause strengthens emotional discipline and calm awareness. In that brief moment of space lies the power to choose how we respond to life.

Emotional sovereignty ultimately means learning to guide your internal world rather than being controlled by external events. Life will always include challenges, uncertainty, and moments of strong emotion, but those experiences do not have to determine your behavior. As the Stoic philosopher Marcus Aurelius wrote, "You have power over your mind—not outside events. Realize this, and you will find strength." When you learn to regulate your responses with awareness and intention, you gain a quiet form of strength that influences every part of your life. Emotional sovereignty is not perfection, but the ongoing practice of responding with clarity, resilience, and calm authority.

Lastly, I want to express my gratitude. Thank you for taking the time to engage with this book and for your commitment to mastery over your emotions. Your courage and effort in taking this step is commendable.

DID YOU KNOW?

Remember the game Red Light, Green Light as a kid?

At the time, it probably just felt like fun—running, stopping, trying not to get caught moving. But what you didn't realize is that you were learning something powerful. Every time you froze on "red light," you were practicing impulse control. Every time you resisted the urge to move too soon, you were training your nervous system to pause instead of react. You were building discipline without even knowing it.

Emotional control works the same way. Life constantly gives you "green lights" and "red lights"—moments where you feel the urge to speak, react, lash out, shut down, or act on impulse. The difference between reacting and responding comes down to one simple skill: the ability to pause.

And most people never master that.

But you already started learning it a long time ago. That moment between what you feel and what you do next—that's your red light. That's where you decide whether your emotions control you, or you control them.

That pause is not weakness.

That pause is power.

And that power is what this entire book has been about.

Every chapter, every insight, every strategy has been leading you to this one truth: emotional sovereignty is not about controlling the world around you—it's about mastering what happens within you. The ability to pause, to become aware, and to choose your response is the foundation of that mastery.

You've had this skill in you all along. Now, you know how to use it.

A Letter to You, the Reader

If you are reading this right now, I want you to pause for a moment.

You made it.

You didn't just pick this book up—you stayed. You read, reflected, questioned, and challenged yourself. And that alone tells me something powerful about you: you are not someone who wants to stay stuck. You are someone who is searching for understanding, for growth, and for control over something most people spend their entire lives avoiding—their own emotions.

That matters more than you probably realize.

Most people never get this far. They live reacting, blaming, suppressing, or escaping what they feel. They allow their emotions to drive their decisions, shape their relationships, and ultimately control their lives without ever stopping to ask why. But you did something different. You chose to look inward. You chose awareness.

And awareness is where everything begins.

The Stoics believed that while we cannot control everything that happens to us, we can control how we respond. This idea is simple, but it is not easy. Life will test you. People will misunderstand you. Situations will arise that feel unfair, overwhelming, or completely out of your control. But within all of that, there is one place where your power always exists—your response.

You are not responsible for everything that has happened to you. But you are responsible for what you choose to do with it.

That is emotional sovereignty.

It is not about becoming emotionless. It is not about suppressing anger, sadness, or fear. It is about understanding those emotions, learning from them, and refusing to let them control your actions. It is about creating space between what you feel and what you choose to do next.

That space is where your power lives.

There will be moments after this book where you forget everything you've read. You will react too quickly, say something you didn't mean, or fall back into old patterns. That does not mean you have failed. It means you are human. Growth is not a straight line—it is a process of awareness, correction, and continued effort.

The goal is not perfection.

The goal is progress.

Every time you pause instead of reacting, you are winning. Every time you choose understanding over assumption, you are growing. Every time you take responsibility for your emotions instead of placing them on someone else, you are stepping into a level of maturity that most people never reach.

This is how you change your life.

Not in one big moment, but in small, consistent decisions.

The Stoics also taught that we should not waste energy on what we cannot control. This includes other people's opinions, actions, and behaviors. You cannot control how others treat you, but you can control how much power you give to it. You cannot control whether someone understands you, but you can control whether you remain grounded in who you are.

When you stop trying to control everything outside of you, you finally gain control of what is within you.

And that is where peace begins.

As you move forward from this book, I want you to carry one truth with you:

You are not your emotions.

You experience them, but they do not define you. They are signals, not commands. They are information, not identity. The moment you understand that is the moment you begin to separate who you are from what you feel.

And that separation is freedom.

There is a version of you that responds instead of reacts. A version of you that does not get pulled into every emotional wave, but instead stands steady, aware, and in control. That version of you is not something you have to become—it is something you uncover.

It has been there all along.

This journey does not end here. In many ways, it is just beginning. The work of emotional mastery is something you will carry into your relationships, your decisions, your challenges, and your growth. It will shape the way you communicate, the way you handle conflict, and the way you show up in your own life.

And over time, if you stay committed to this path, you will notice something powerful.

You will feel more grounded.

More clear.

More in control.

Not because life became easier—but because you became stronger.

So as you close this book, don't just walk away from it.

Carry it with you.

Practice what you've learned. Reflect on your patterns. Be honest with yourself. Give yourself grace when you fall short, but never lose sight of the direction you are moving in.

Because the fact that you made it this far tells me something I don't say lightly:

You are capable of mastering your emotions.

And when you do that…

You don't just change your reactions.

You change your life.

"The happiness of your life depends upon the quality of your thoughts." ~ Marcus Aurelius

—My Best Regards,

Deborah E. Jones

Recommended Apps for Emotional Regulation

Modern technology can be a powerful ally in emotional self-regulation. The following apps offer tools such as mindfulness training, cognitive-behavioral therapy exercises, mood tracking, breathing techniques, and guided meditation. While these tools do not replace professional therapy, they can support daily emotional awareness and reinforce the practices discussed throughout this book.

1. Headspace – Mindfulness & Meditation

🌐 https://www.headspace.com

Headspace is one of the most widely used mindfulness apps in the world. It provides guided meditations, stress-reduction exercises, sleep support, and short breathing sessions designed to calm the nervous system. Research has shown that mindfulness programs like Headspace can help reduce stress and anxiety when practiced regularly.

2. Calm – Meditation, Sleep & Relaxation

🌐 https://www.calm.com

Calm is designed to help users relax, reduce anxiety, and improve sleep through guided meditation and breathing exercises. It also includes soothing music, "sleep stories," and mindfulness sessions that help users slow down racing thoughts and regulate emotional responses.

3. MindShift CBT – Cognitive Behavioral Therapy Tools

🌐 https://www.anxietycanada.com/resources/mindshift-cbt/

MindShift CBT is a free app based on Cognitive Behavioral Therapy (CBT) principles. It helps users manage anxiety, challenge negative thoughts, and build healthier thinking patterns. The app includes mood tracking, goal setting, relaxation exercises, and tools for confronting fears gradually.

4. Woebot – AI Emotional Support Chatbot

🌐 https://woebothealth.com

Woebot is an AI-powered chatbot designed to help users process emotions using techniques drawn from CBT and mindfulness. The app checks in with users daily and offers guided conversations that teach emotional awareness and coping strategies. Studies have shown that regular use can help reduce symptoms of depression and anxiety.

5. MoodMission – Action-Based Emotional Coping

🌐 https://moodmission.com

MoodMission recommends small practical "missions" based on how you're feeling. For example, if you report anxiety or low mood, the app suggests simple actions such as breathing exercises, grounding techniques, or physical activity to help regulate emotions.

6. Moodfit – Emotional Health Tracking

🌐 https://www.getmoodfit.com

Moodfit focuses on helping users understand emotional patterns over time. It combines journaling, mindfulness practices, and CBT-based tools with mood tracking so users can identify triggers and behavioral trends that affect emotional well-being.

Using Technology as a Tool for Inner Work

Emotional sovereignty ultimately comes from self-awareness and consistent practice. Apps like these can provide structure, reminders, and guided exercises that reinforce emotional regulation skills. Digital tools can help individuals track their emotions, practice mindfulness, and recognize patterns in their reactions, making it easier to apply the principles discussed throughout this book.

When used intentionally, these resources can support the inner work required to strengthen emotional awareness, build resilience, and cultivate calm clarity in everyday life.

YouTube Videos for Emotional Regulation

Video learning can be a powerful way to reinforce the practices discussed in this book. The following videos provide guided exercises, breathing techniques, and psychological strategies that support emotional awareness and self-regulation.

1.   Breathing Techniques for Emotional Control https://www.youtube.com/watch?v=rPXuhXndOZc

2.   Dialectical Behavior Therapy (DBT) Emotion Regulation Skills https://www.youtube.com/watch?v=T7Sc8jpbAgA

3.   Guided Meditation for Emotional Regulation https://www.youtube.com/watch?v=hiEcUotdvBQ

4.   Mindfulness Meditation for Observing Emotions https://www.youtube.com/watch?v=rrXmjeUdzeM

5.   Grounding Exercise for Anxiety and Emotional Overwhelm https://www.youtube.com/watch?v=30VMIEmA114

6.   Breathwork for Nervous System Regulation https://www.youtube.com/watch?v=kPYuUzfi268

Using Video Resources for Emotional Mastery

Educational videos can reinforce the emotional regulation skills discussed throughout this book. Practices such as breathing exercises, mindfulness meditation, grounding techniques, and cognitive behavioral strategies help individuals build awareness and strengthen emotional resilience over time.

Consistent practice is key. Even a few minutes of daily mindfulness or breathing exercises can help train the brain to respond more calmly to emotional triggers and stressful situations.

Influential Thinkers in Emotional Regulation and Emotional Mastery

The concept of emotional sovereignty draws from centuries of philosophical thought and decades of psychological research. The following thinkers, researchers, and authors have made significant contributions to understanding how individuals can regulate emotions, develop resilience, and cultivate inner stability.

Marcus Aurelius

One of the most well-known Stoic philosophers, Marcus Aurelius, emphasized the power individuals have over their thoughts and responses. His writings in Meditations continue to inspire readers to focus on controlling their internal world rather than external events.

Epictetus

Epictetus taught that suffering often comes from our judgments about events rather than the events themselves. His teachings on self-discipline and emotional control laid the philosophical foundation for modern cognitive behavioral therapy.

Seneca

Seneca wrote extensively about anger, emotional restraint, and rational thinking. His work emphasized the importance of examining emotional impulses before acting upon them.

Aaron T. Beck

Aaron Beck developed Cognitive Behavioral Therapy (CBT), a psychological approach that helps individuals identify and reshape thought patterns that influence emotional responses.

Albert Ellis

Albert Ellis introduced Rational Emotive Behavior Therapy (REBT), which teaches that emotional distress is often caused by irrational beliefs and interpretations rather than the events themselves.

Daniel Goleman

Daniel Goleman popularized the concept of emotional intelligence through his bestselling book Emotional Intelligence. His work highlighted the importance of self-awareness, emotional regulation, and empathy in personal and professional success.

Jon Kabat-Zinn

Jon Kabat-Zinn developed Mindfulness-Based Stress Reduction (MBSR), a widely studied program that teaches individuals how to observe thoughts and emotions with awareness rather than reacting automatically.

Brené Brown

Brené Brown's research on vulnerability, courage, and emotional resilience has helped millions understand the importance of emotional awareness and authentic self-expression.

James Gross

James Gross is a leading researcher in the field of emotion regulation. His work explores how individuals manage emotional responses and how different strategies influence psychological well-being.

Viktor Frankl

Viktor Frankl's work in Man's Search for Meaning emphasized that even in the most difficult circumstances, individuals retain the power to choose their attitude and response to suffering.

Continuing the Work of Emotional Sovereignty

The thinkers listed above represent a long tradition of philosophical and psychological inquiry into emotional self-mastery. Their teachings emphasize a shared principle: while we cannot control every event in life, we can learn to guide our responses with awareness and intention.

Emotional sovereignty builds upon this tradition by integrating philosophical insight with modern psychological practices, encouraging individuals to develop clarity, resilience, and calm authority in their everyday lives.

References

Online Articles and Publications

American Psychological Association. (n.d.). Emotion regulation.

https://www.apa.org

Anxiety Canada. (n.d.). MindShift CBT: Anxiety management tools.

https://www.anxietycanada.com

Gross, J. J. (2015). Emotion regulation: Current status and future prospects. Psychological Inquiry.

https://doi.org/10.1080/1047840X.2014.940781

Harvard Health Publishing. (2020). Mindfulness meditation may ease anxiety and mental stress.

https://www.health.harvard.edu

Kabat-Zinn, J. (2019). Mindfulness-based stress reduction and emotional regulation. Mindfulness Journal.

https://link.springer.com

National Institute of Mental Health. (n.d.). Managing stress and emotional well-being.

https://www.nimh.nih.gov

Books

Beck, A. T. (2011). Cognitive therapy: Basics and beyond. Guilford Press.

Brown, B. (2018). Dare to lead: Brave work, tough conversations, whole hearts. Random House.

Ellis, A. (1994). Reason and emotion in psychotherapy. Citadel Press.

Frankl, V. (2006). Man's search for meaning. Beacon Press.

Goleman, D. (1995). Emotional intelligence: Why it can matter more than IQ. Bantam Books.

Kabat-Zinn, J. (1994). Wherever you go, there you are: Mindfulness meditation in everyday life. Hyperion.

Miller, J. (2004). A brief introduction to stoicism. Oxford University Press.

Pigliucci, M. (2017). How to be a stoic: Using ancient philosophy to live a modern life. Basic Books.

Robertson, D. (2019). How to think like a Roman emperor: The Stoic philosophy of Marcus Aurelius. St. Martin's Press.

Case Studies and Research

Gross, J. J. (1998). The emerging field of emotion regulation: An integrative review. Review of General Psychology.

Keng, S. L., Smoski, M. J., & Robins, C. J. (2011). Effects of mindfulness on psychological health: A review of empirical studies. Clinical Psychology Review.

Hofmann, S. G., Sawyer, A. T., Witt, A. A., & Oh, D. (2010). The effect of mindfulness-based therapy on anxiety and depression. Journal of Consulting and Clinical Psychology.

Davidson, R. J., & McEwen, B. S. (2012). Social influences on neuroplasticity: Stress and interventions to promote well-being. Nature Neuroscience.

Linehan, M. (2015). Dialectical behavior therapy for emotional regulation. Behavior Research and Therapy.